FANTASTIC SPORTS FACTS

BASKETBALL

Michael Hurley

Chicago, Illinois

© 2013 Raintree
an imprint of Capstone Global Library, LLC
Chicago, Illinois

All rights reserved. No part of this publication may be
reproduced or transmitted in any form or by any means,
electronic or mechanical, including photocopying, recording,
taping, or any information storage and retrieval system,
without permission in writing from the publisher.

Edited by Catherine Veitch, Sian Smith,
  and John-Paul Wilkins
Designed by Richard Parker
Original illustrations © Capstone Global Library Ltd 2013
Picture research by Ruth Blair
Originated by Capstone Global Library Ltd
Printed in the United States of America in
North Mankato, Minnesota

042014
008162RP

Library of Congress Cataloging-in-Publication Data
Cataloging-in-Publication data is available at the Library
of Congress.
ISBN 978-1-4109-5104-5 (hbk)
ISBN 978-1-4109-5111-3 (pbk)

Acknowledgments
We would like to thank the following for permission to
reproduce photographs: Corbis pp. 10 (© Leon T Switzer/
ZUMA Press), 13 (© Larry W. Smith/epa), 19 (© Bettmann),
20 (© Dimitri Iundt/TempSport), 21 (© Erich Schlegel/
Dallas Morning News), 26 (© Chris Trotman/PCN); Getty
Images pp. 7, 17 (Focus On Sport), 15 (Christian Petersen), 18
(Hulton Archive), 22 (David E. Klutho/Sports Illustrated), 23
(David E. Klutho/Sports Illustrated), 24 (JEFF HAYNES/AFP),
25 (James Drake /Sports Illustrated), 27 (Sports Illustrated);
Photoshot pp. 8, 9 (© Imago), 14 (Icon SMI); Shutterstock
pp. 4 (© Mayskyphoto), 5 (© Doug James), 9 (© Vlue), 12 (©
DVARG), 14 (© vovan), 16 (© Alhovik); Superstock p. 11 (©
imagebroker.net).

Front cover photograph of Lisa Leslie reproduced with
permission of Corbis (© Darryl Dennis/Icon SMI), and
a basketball reproduced with permission of Shutterstock
(© Picsfive).

Every effort has been made to contact copyright holders
of any material reproduced in this book. Any omissions
will be rectified in subsequent printings if notice is given
to the publisher.

Disclaimer
All the Internet addresses (URLs) given in this book were
valid at the time of going to press. However, due to the
dynamic nature of the Internet, some addresses may have
changed, or sites may have changed or ceased to exist since
publication. While the author and publisher regret any
inconvenience this may cause readers, no responsibility
for any such changes can be accepted by either the author
or the publisher.

Contents

Some words are printed in bold, **like this**. You can find out what they mean by looking in the glossary.

Basketball Basics

The most popular basketball league in the world is the NBA, based in the United States. The best players from around the world play in the NBA.

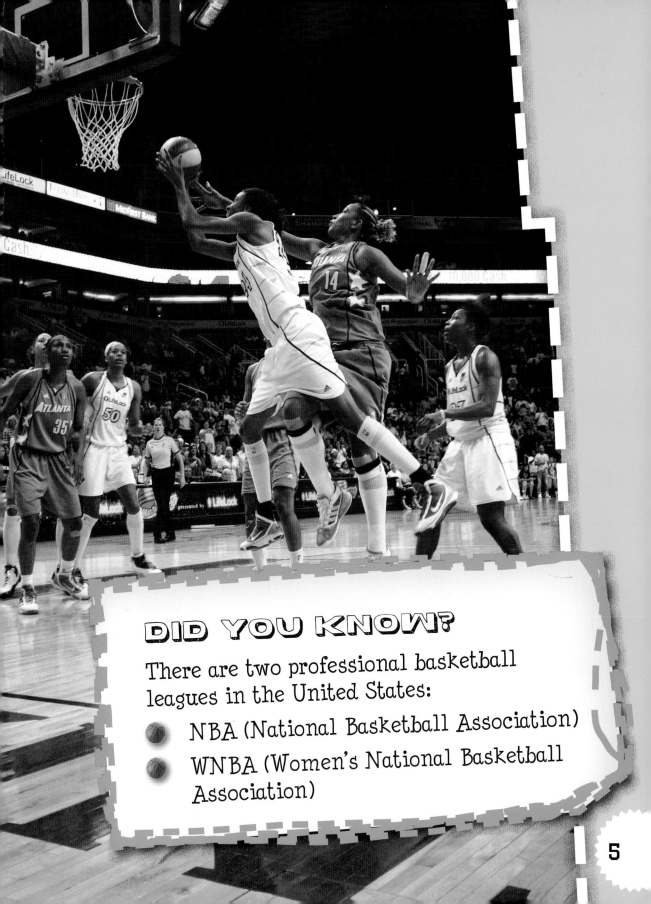

DID YOU KNOW?

There are two professional basketball leagues in the United States:
- NBA (National Basketball Association)
- WNBA (Women's National Basketball Association)

Highest-Scoring Game

The highest-scoring game in NBA history was played between the Detroit Pistons and Denver Nuggets in December 1983. Detroit won, with a final score of 186–184.

Isiah Thomas was the top scorer for Detroit, with 47 points.

DID YOU KNOW?

The lowest-scoring game at the Olympics took place in 1936. The United States beat Canada 19-8. The game was played outdoors, in the rain!

Lucky Shorts

Many basketball players are **superstitious**. **Legendary** player Michael Jordan always wore a pair of his old college shorts beneath his playing shorts, for good luck.

FUN FACT

Before Jason Terry plays a team, he gets a pair of the team's shorts. He wears them to bed the night before the game for good luck!

Most Famous Team

The most famous basketball team in the world is the Harlem Globetrotters. The Globetrotters do not play in any league. They travel all over the world to play in **exhibition** games.

The Harlem
Globetrotters
WOW
the crowds with
amazing **dribbling**, passing,
and shooting tricks!

Unusual World Record

Dwight Howard was rewarded with a new world record during the NBA **All-Star** Weekend in 2010. He made a shot from over the half-court line. The incredible thing was that Howard sat down to take the shot!

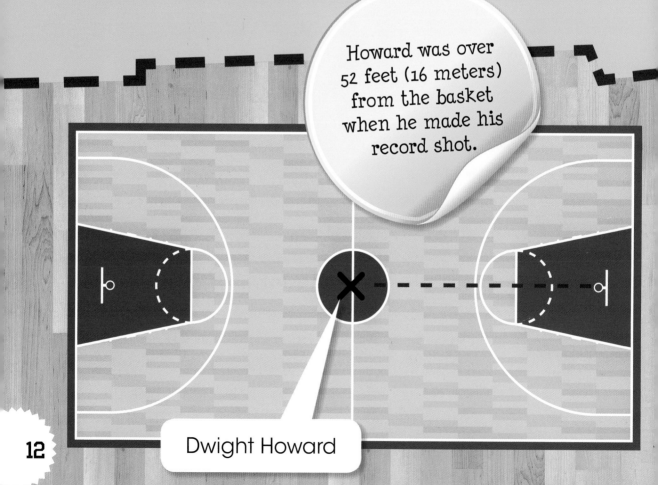

Howard was over 52 feet (16 meters) from the basket when he made his record shot.

Dwight Howard

FUN FACT

In 2008, Dwight Howard won the All-Star **Slam Dunk** Contest while wearing a Superman cape!

Highest Earners

Kobe Bryant is the highest-paid player in the NBA. He plays for the Los Angeles Lakers. Bryant earns over $25 million a year! He has helped the Lakers to win five NBA championships.

DID YOU KNOW?

One of the top players in the WNBA, Candace Parker, plays for the Los Angeles Sparks and is paid around $100,000 per year.

This table shows the top five highest-paid NBA players:

Player	Team	Pay
Kobe Bryant	Los Angeles Lakers	$25.2m
Rashard Lewis	Washington Wizards	$22.1m
Tim Duncan	San Antonio Spurs	$21.3m
Kevin Garnett	Boston Celtics	$21.2m
Dirk Nowitzki	Dallas Mavericks	$19.0m

Time Testers

The longest game in NBA history took place in 1951. The Indiana Olympians beat the Rochester Royals. The game lasted for 78 minutes, which is 30 minutes longer than a normal game!

01 : 18 : 00
HRS   MINS   SECS

RECORD BREAKERS

In 2007, a basketball game in Romania lasted for an incredible 80 hours. That is more than three days! The players set a new world record for the longest basketball game ever.

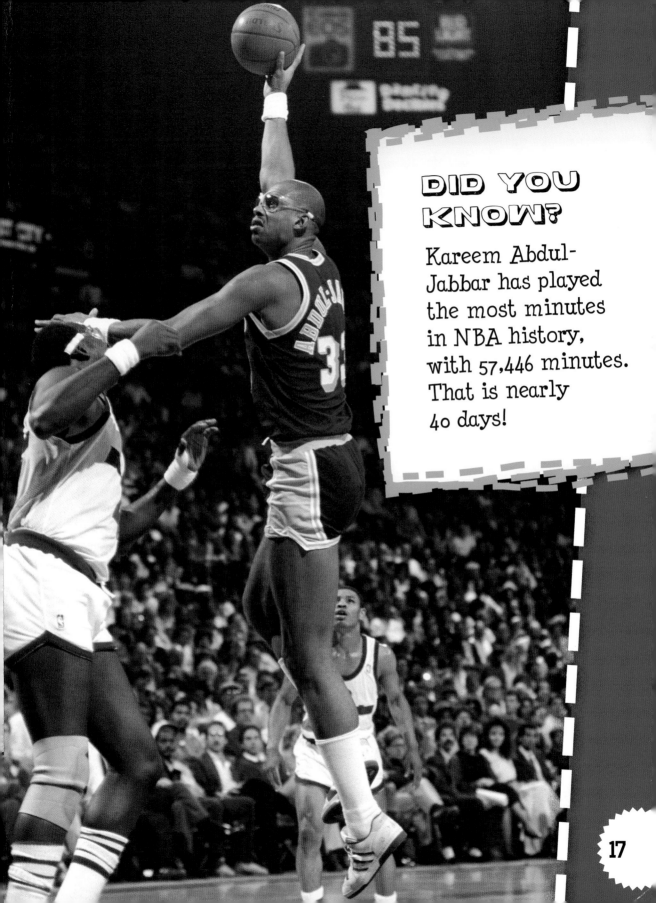

DID YOU KNOW?

Kareem Abdul-Jabbar has played the most minutes in NBA history, with 57,446 minutes. That is nearly 40 days!

Origins of Basketball

Naismith is pictured here with his basketball team in 1891.

Basketball was invented in 1891 in Massachusetts by a sports coach named James Naismith. It only took him two weeks to come up with the new sport!

Naismith used a soccer ball and a peach basket for early basketball games.

RECORD BREAKERS

The document on which Naismith wrote down the original 13 rules of basketball sold for an incredible $4.3 million in 2010. This set a world record for sports **memorabilia**.

Dream Team

For the 1992 Olympics, the United States put together the greatest basketball team in history. The team was full of top NBA stars. It was known as the "Dream Team." The team won the gold medal, winning all of its games.

FUN FACT

The "Dream Team" beat opponents by an **average** of 44 points per game!

DID YOU KNOW?

The U.S. women's basketball team has won the gold medal at the last four Olympics.

Tallest and Shortest

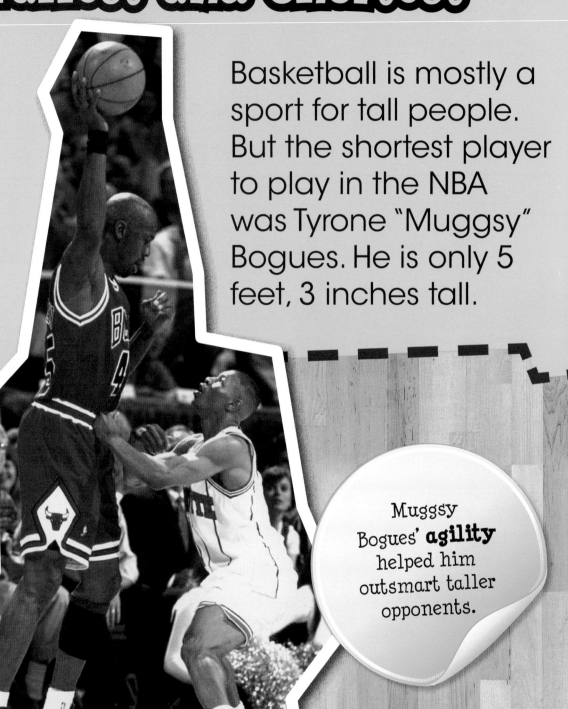

Basketball is mostly a sport for tall people. But the shortest player to play in the NBA was Tyrone "Muggsy" Bogues. He is only 5 feet, 3 inches tall.

Muggsy Bogues' **agility** helped him outsmart taller opponents.

RECORD BREAKERS

The tallest player in NBA history was Manute Bol (pictured left). He was an amazing 7 feet, 7 inches tall.

FUN FACT

The tallest basketball player in Olympic history is Libyan Suleiman Ali Nashnush. He is over 8 feet tall!

Great Players

The most successful basketball player of all time is Michael Jordan. The Chicago Bulls star holds the record for the highest scoring **average** in NBA history, with 31.0 points per game.

Nancy Lieberman is one of the best ever female basketball players. In 1986, she became the first woman to join a men's professional team.

DID YOU KNOW?

Lieberman was the youngest ever winner of an Olympic medal for basketball, playing for the United States. She was just 18.

Leslie was a very important member of the gold medal-winning U.S. basketball teams in four Olympics.

Lisa Leslie is one of the greatest female basketball players in history. She won the WNBA championship with her team, the Los Angeles Sparks.

Larry Bird was a basketball superstar. He played for the Boston Celtics for 13 seasons between 1979 and 1992. He won three straight regular-season **MVP** awards from 1984 to 1986.

DID YOU KNOW?

In his **rookie** season, Larry Bird led the Celtics in scoring, **rebounds**, **steals**, and minutes played.

Quiz

Are you a superfan or a couch potato? Decide whether the statements below are true or false. Then look at the answers on page 31 and check your score on the fanometer.

1 Derrick Rose is the youngest ever winner of the NBA **MVP** award.

2 The Chicago Bulls have won the most NBA championship titles.

3 A soccer ball was used in early basketball games.

TOP TIP
Some of the answers can be found in this book, but you may have to find some yourself.

4 The Olympic match between the United States and Canada in 1936 was played outside.

5 Kobe Bryant has won four NBA Championships with the Los Angeles Lakers.

6 Michael Jordan scored an **average** of 31.0 points per game.

FANOMETER

fair-weather fan

couch potato

superfan

1 2 3 4 5 6

Glossary

agility ability to move quickly and easily

all-star made up of the best players

average sum of adding two or more numbers together and dividing by the number of numbers

dribble move along while bouncing the ball

exhibition collection of things put on display for people to look at

legendary very famous

memorabilia objects that are kept or collected to remember something by

MVP short for "most valuable player"

rebound act of catching the ball after it has bounced off the backboard or rim

rookie sports player in his or her first year

slam dunk push the ball forcefully through the basketball hoop from above

steal gain possession of the ball from an opponent

superstitious having a belief that is not based on reason or evidence

Find Out More

Books

Gifford, Clive. *Basketball* (Know Your Sport). Mankato, Minn.: Sea-to-Sea, 2010.

Slade, Suzanne. *Basketball: How It Works* (Science of Sports). Mankato, Minn.: Capstone, 2010.

Websites

Facthound offers a safe, fun way to find Internet sites related to this book. All of the sites on Facthound have been researched by our staff.

Here's all you do:

Visit www.facthound.com

Type in this code: 9781410951045

Quiz answers

1) True. Rose won the MVP award in 2011, at the age of 22.
2) False. Boston has won the most NBA Championships, with 17 titles.
3) True (see page 19).
4) True (see page 7).
5) False. Bryant has won five NBA Championships with the Los Angeles Lakers (see page 14)
6) True (see page 24).

Index

JUL 08 2014